GW01402938

TIME, TUNA,

and Other Tales:

HUMOROUS REFLECTIONS ON MARRIAGE, MOTHERHOOD, AND MORE

GINA T. BROADBENT

Time, Tuna, and Other Tales:
Humorous Reflections on Marriage, Motherhood, and More,
is a work of nonfiction. Some names and identifying
details have been changed.

Copyright ©2024 by Gina T. Broadbent
Avon, Connecticut

No part of this book may be reproduced in any manner
without written permission from the publisher.

All rights reserved.

Published by Catherine R. Broadbent
in the United States of America with IngramSpark.

Library of Congress Cataloging-In-Publication Data:

Names: Broadbent, Gina T., Author
Title: Time, Tuna, and Other Tales: Humorous Reflections on Marriage,
Motherhood, and More / Gina T. Broadbent

Identifiers:
Library of Congress Control Number: 2024925002
ISBN: 979-8-9918281-1-6

Genre: Wit and Humor/Personal Memoirs;
Essays; Family and Relationships;
Motherhood, and Life

A Gina T. Broadbent Book
Printed in the United States of America

Cover and book design by Cheryl Gioielli
Gioielli-Design.com

To Catherine and Jeff

for your never-ending inspiration,
laughter, and love.

contents

Wrapping It Up

I've never been good at estimating time. It was ten or maybe fifteen years ago when I joined a writers' group. A dozen middle-aged women shared their ambitious attempts toward literary stardom. Three published authors assumed dimly disguised roles of good cop, bad cop, and justice of the peace as they critiqued submissions. My fellow participants wrote memoirs of childhood trauma, forays into young-adult angst, and fictionalizations of "ripped from the headlines" murder mysteries. Cowed by their gravitas, I sheepishly contributed fluffy vignettes about family and friends, pastimes and pet peeves.

To my surprise and smidge of satisfaction, my musings on the ups and downs of the low-carb lifestyle or my husband's questionable wardrobe choices captured my colleagues' attention. They chuckled, guffawed, and occasionally shed tears of laughter. The group leaders urged me to create a blog, believing that my stories perfectly fit the parameters of the latest literary genre. My work was informal, short, esoteric, and, in one coach's estimation, always tied up with a pretty little bow.

I wasted no time, buying a prophetically named domain: "Coulda Shoulda Woulda." Ten or maybe fifteen years of the minutiae of everyday life delayed the birth of my blog. I probably coulda have written, certainly shoulda written, and absolutely woulda written.

But time flew. Trite, true, and tinged with sadness, as my domain name expired, I learned that my own end date loomed as well.

I now assess the passage of time with far more precision, no longer casually dismissing its duration as ten or maybe fifteen years, weeks, days, or hours. I do not rue the elusive "coulda shoulda woulda." Instead, I reflect on the enduring "done that, seen that, been there". Even my frivolous essays from ten or maybe fifteen years ago warrant a glance. Do any of the topics on which I once waxed poetic remain relevant or remotely funny?

I am amazed to find that the answer is yes, and yes. Many of my subjects survive the test of time. My husband's achievement of sartorial splendor continues to rival pursuit of the Holy Grail. [*"Dressing Daddy"*]. Post-pandemic safeguards guarantee that the suggestion of Purell flowing from baptismal fonts is but a wee bit neurotic. [*"Fan-tastic Fears!"*] My hair has fallen out twice. I find it poignant, although not pointless, to read my rants about kinky curls and the misogynists who tried to tame them. [*"Harried"*]. Awake or asleep [*"Past My Bedtime"*], my unfulfilled dream of a hole-in-one never dies [*"Another Four-Letter Word"*]. And who could predict that my confession of claustrophobia would live on as a relevant, albeit macabre, contemplation? [*"Fan-tastic Fears!"*]

It's time to wrap it up, never forgetting that pretty little bow.

GINA T. BROADBENT

A Blog By Any Other Name

Blog - it's *the* thing to do. Write a blog, read a blog, follow a blog. Since I've used "blog" five times in my first twenty, it may be hard to believe that I do not like this word, blog. But just say "blog." It does not roll off the tongue; rather, it gets caught in the esophagus like half-chewed steak. Listen to "blog". It resembles the sound made after washing down a bad fried clam with one tequila too many. Think about "blog." It brings to mind the dregs of dirt and debris on the Bronx to Brooklyn subway. Blog is a downright ugly word.

While I am queasy about the sight and sound of the "b" word [Sorry, just can't utter it again, not so soon after the clam, tequila, and subway sediment images], there is a flip side to "blog" [Oops, I said it again!]. Blog is a portmanteau. Portmanteau is a word I quite enjoy. It trips from the lips like a tender kiss, lands upon the ears like a Debussy waltz, evokes a picnic of brie and Bordeaux beneath a willow in the Loire Valley. It holds within it romance, melody, mystery. If I snap out of my sappy reverie long enough, I will admit that the primary definition of portmanteau [love that word!] is suitcase. Whatever romance is associated with "suitcase" depends upon its destination; Paris, oh, yes; Portland, not so much; Peoria, oh, no. But the secondary definition of portmanteau is far more alluring: "a blending of two or more distinct forms."

This conjures thoughts of, must I be explicit?, romance at its most basic level.

Blog [It's becoming a bit easier to say] is the intermarriage of two words, web and log. Leave the "w" and "e" behind, cozy the "b" right up against the "log" to create "blog." Blog joins a panoply of portmanteaux. Some, like infomercial, telethon, brunch, and smog, are so commonplace that I am left to slap the palm of my hand to my forehead exclaiming "It's a portmanteau, stupid!" Some have lives of their own. Sarah Palin may be best remembered for her invention of the gem "refudiate" when she combined refute with repudiate. I appreciate creativity, which, coupled with incessant laughing, may be a necessary characteristic for any vice president. Sarah got into a jam when she compared herself to Shakespeare, who apparently dropped portmanteaux all over the place. She refused to refudiate "refudiate." Some portmanteaux have multiple, albeit short, lives; think Bennifer. Some have inevitable deaths: Brangelina. Need I say more?

If blog is simply a made-up word, why can't I come up with a word that means the same thing but doesn't make me gag? Why can't I pack my own portmanteau? I have thought long and hard. In fact, I thought about it most of last summer. I worked on it at the beach. "Want to go for a swim?" "Thanks, but, no, I'm working on my portmanteau." Friends stared at me, contemplating the greater risk: to stay on the sand with a lunatic like me or to dive head first into the shark-infested Cape Cod waters. I worked on it on the golf course as I, personifying portmanteau, paraded about in a skort. I even worked on it at work, which not only did nothing for the already struggling gross national product but also made me late for a teleconference. [Time to slap my forehead again!]

I thought about "binfo", combining web and info. My inner feminist objected. Binfo sounds a tad too much like bimbo. I thought about "webin," another blend of web and info. I shied away, haunted by a vision of little duck feet sticking out of my portmanteau. I thought about "bessay," mixing web and essay.

Bessay? What can I say? Only that a blog by any other name would read the same.

GINA T. BROADBENT

A Mother's Job Is Never Done

As the cardinal rule of motherhood states, "If you don't embarrass your child, you're not doing your job."

I've always been a bit of an overachiever, and never more so than during my daughter's tween/teen years. I pursued with passion such as that I usually reserve for a crisp sauvignon blanc or a deep-tissue massage, perfection on this compass of parental competence. I did everything to ensure a roll of her eyes, a highly offended yelp of "EWWW," and the ultimate utterance, "Mom, people heard you say that!" Here are some of my strategies.

I sang. My daughter has never been a fan of my singing. When she was a toddler, I sang her to sleep every night [or so I thought]. My repertoire gave a nod to her multi-ethnic heritage; "When Irish Eyes are Smiling," "Edelweiss," and, of course, "Volare," until one evening, when she pressed her chubby, two-year-old fingers against my lips and pleaded, "No, Mama, no!" Undeterred, I sang at every chance, at home, at church, and, most grievously, in the car with her middle–school friends in the backseat. I am not sure what bothered her most; my ever so slightly off-key mezzo soprano or the fact I was so blissfully "uncool." I am not sure when the stifled snickers began; when I tuned in to WJMJ [W Jesus Mary and Joseph, our local Catholic easy-listening station], when I sang along with Josh Groban, or when, grooving on Josh, I started to snap my fingers. I am sure, since we mothers all have eyes in the back of our heads, that my daughter rolled her eyes.

I attended every school event. The term "helicopter parent" was coined in my town. Mothers trampled over one another to land the highly coveted roles: room mother, cookie mom, field trip chaperone. Warding off investigation by the Department of Children and Family Services for neglect, my fellow moms and I were on hand for every basketball game, choral concert, and cut-throat math club competition.

My daughter could not complain about my perfect attendance record, opting instead to critique my not-so-perfect appearance. When I walked through the school doors in my twin sweater set and pencil skirt, my daughter wished for a mom who could/would rock a denim mini and spaghetti strap tank from Forever 21. Her comment, "EWWW, Talbots!"

I asked "that" question. There are some questions that parents should never ask because they already know the answer. Merely posing them brings unmitigated shame and potential social exile to a child. I, however, couldn't stop myself.

"Will the mom be home to chaperone the party?"

"Of course, Mom!"

Of course, when I dropped my daughter off, the aforementioned parent was always in the shower; otherwise she'd be delighted to come and say hello. I assumed she was so busy showering that she didn't have a chance to pick up the stash of red Solo cups that littered her front lawn.

I moved to a more provocative question in the pre-college years. On every campus tour, I asked, "Is this a co-ed dorm?" As the smiling admissions rep, failing to recognize the rhetorical nature of my inquiry, launched into a well-practiced litany about independent living, the value of diversity, and finding oneself, my daughter launched into her own well-practiced litany; eye roll, EWWW, and worst of all, "Mom, people heard you ask that!"

As my daughter approached her mid-twenties, I began to wonder if I was falling down on the job. I no longer seemed to be a constant source of embarrassment. She asked to borrow my Talbot's credit card because there were "some nice things there." [Eye roll, this time from me.]

She still frowned upon my singing, but my choice of music was no longer humiliating. In fact, she recommended a few Frank Sinatra songs to me because he is "just the best" and told me about the band she wanted to see in concert, Fleetwood Mac.

So, is yesterday gone? Not all the way. My daughter now is married, but I continue to perform my motherly function.

In a trendy New York City restaurant, I rummaged through my purse to look for some necessary item – tissue, cell phone, credit card – only to be stopped short. "Mom, you look like a tourist. People can see you doing that!" [Eye roll, again from me.]

Dressing Daddy

At the start of our marriage, the following were my husband's five rules of fashion.

1. **Beige is good; more beige is better, and a whole lot of beige is best.**

Most people identify red or green or even periwinkle as their favorite color. Not my husband, Jeff, who liked that nebulous not-brown, not-white shade of regurgitated oatmeal known as beige. He liked it so much that in the pre-Gina era, 90 percent of his wardrobe was beige. He had it all: beige golf shirts, beige [aka khaki] pants, beige sports jacket, even beige socks, all of which he wore simultaneously for an effect that was, at best, underwhelming. There was an advantage [if one can call it that] to Jeff's love affair with beige; his outfits never clashed. No danger of pink paired with red, no maroon mixed with orange. Only beige, bleak and boring beige.

2. **Monotone is a fashion statement.**

Rule #2 is a corollary of rule #1. Even Mr. Beige took an occasional walk on the wild side to venture into a new and exotic place, the world of monotone. With a giant fashion step forward, he sported black with black [think Johnny Cash], brown with brown [think UPS], or my personal favorite, gray with gray [think Ralph Kramden].

All that "matchy matchy" left me screaming for a hint of color, the slightest bit of contrast. "Jeff, don't you think a navy jacket would look nice with the gray pants? Maybe a white shirt? Or a patterned tie?" I was desperate. "Can't you at least break up all that black? Surely you have a beige sweater!"

3. A sweat suit is a go-to outfit for all occasions, except for your grandmother's funeral and possibly your own.

Jeff would choose an appendectomy without anesthesia over donning a jacket, dress shirt, and, worst of all, tie. While the sweat suit offered the obvious allure of an ever-expandable waist and non-existent fit, my husband's steadfast adherence to the aforementioned rules #1 and #2 of his "fashion" code was the root cause for his disdain for a blazer, button-down Oxford shirt, and paisley tie. What could be better than a dyed-to-match Fruit of the Loom sweat suit to maintain the monotone look? What could be sweeter than a dyed-to-match Fruit of the Loom sweat suit in the ever-classic shade of beige...boring beige?

4. White socks, worn with flip flops, are acceptable.

Picture it. Standard drug store $1.99 rubber flip flops accented with white cotton tube socks. Like a dirty little family secret, I struggled to keep Jeff's most grievous fashion faux pas private. But, oh no, every Saturday and Sunday morning, he rolled out of bed, tugged on white high socks, and slipped on flip flops. Sauntering out to the mailbox, in front of

God and the world, he picked up the newspaper; his idea of perfection from head to toe, rocking the flip flop sock look by adding a baseball cap – a beige baseball cap.

5.   Real men don't wear baby blue.

Jeff had a complete aversion to the color baby blue. While never reneging on his allegiance to beige, he would half-heartedly wear royal blue, navy, or sapphire, especially in tandem for that coveted monotone look. At a loss to explain his resistance to baby blue, I was certain that this color was the perfect complement to his complexion. I did not prevail. The baby blue hue was banned from his closet. Not a single thread; no baby blue shirt, tie, or even sweat suit.

Decades of marriage to a woman who is on a first name basis with the entire staff at Talbot's changes a man. It's slow at first. A red plaid shirt here. A green argyle sweater there. Out with the beige and in with the burgundy. Good-bye sweat suit, hello cords and turtleneck.

The transformation of Mr. Beige speeds up when the one child, a daughter, arrives, all but emerging from the womb with a hair bow and J. Crew outfit. In her teen years, she signed up for the cause "Help Dress Daddy." How could he refuse to wear the golf shirts his little girl chose for him, the turquoise, the pink, the tangerine?

Thirty-five years have passed. The following now are Jeff Broadbent's two rules of fashion.

1. **Lay out my clothes for me.**

In an effort to get dressed only once before going out, Jeff has agreed to wear just about anything we choose for him. Well, just about anything...

2. **Real men don't wear baby blue.**

Harried

For the first ten years of my life, I was oblivious to the fact that my kinky brown hair went every which way at once, rising above my forehead like over-beaten meringue – only darker. The double helix of my Mediterranean DNA deemed it inevitable that I would be "blessed" with a mass of curly locks. My Italian father, with a mane of thick waves, and my Sicilian mother, with perfect, face-framing ringlets, never wrestled with two terrors, frizz and kink, which would torture me. How could they not be delighted that their baby daughter, their little Shirley Temple, was born with so many curls that the pediatric nurses put a bow in my hair? Little did anyone know that the perfect storm lay ahead, when pre-pubescence, mean boys, and the 1960s would collide.

Enter Paulie Poopalotti, the quintessential fifth-grade bully. Wiry and skinny, with a perpetual smirk, Paulie lived life at the top of his lungs, tormenting anyone who crossed his path. My path crossed with Paulie's just a little too often. He reveled in chasing me home from school, calling out his pet names for me from a safe distance on the opposite side of the street. "Hey, "tapig nose, how's your brillo head?" While neither "tapig nose" nor "brillo head" was a term of endearment, "tapig nose" did not bother me. In the midst of middle-school misery, I realized that even a half brain like Paulie Poopalotti could be clever; after all, my last name was Tapogna. But Barbara Streisand and I had something in common, and it was not a voice like a bell. So brillo head stung. To Paulie Poopalotti, I resembled not a precocious child star but rather the wire-like pad dripping with milky blue soap that my mother used to scrub off dried fried egg. It was my hair, my coiled, corkscrew hair that set me apart from the other girls, Susie, Diane, and Patty (or as Paulie called them Susie-Q, Di-licious, and Patty Cakes). Their straight, blonde tresses hung like undercooked linguini, while I sported a casserole of re-heated rotini upon my head.

The sixty-year war had begun. It was Gina vs. hair for six decades fraught with futile strategies, fruitless battles, and frustrating defeats. While young Mr. Poopalotti's taunts were the immediate cause of conflict, it was the times (they were a-changing) that underlay the whole ongoing brouhaha. In the mid-1960s, at least one glossy news magazine per week slipped through the Tapogna mail slot, featuring Twiggy with her pin-straight boy cut or a "mod" model with long slick hair parted right down the middle. The Woodstock generation stripped off their clothes in protest of everything Establishment, but they still chanted about their crowning glory. "Long beautiful hair, shining, gleaming, streaming, flaxen, waxen...long as God can grow it my hair."

I built an arsenal of weapons for a direct assault on my arch enemy, curl. I amassed ammo; bonnet dryer, blow dryer, foam, wire, and hot rollers, and the ultimate armament, an oversized juice can. When the heavy artillery failed, I forged a path of subterfuge, applying balms, bromides, and pomades. My battle was relentless; escalating from middle school to high school to "damn the torpedoes full steam ahead" by college. Night after night, I waged a sneak attack on my frizzy foe. I blew-dry my hair, nearly pulling it out of its follicles, as I wound it around a brush, whose diameter rivaled the planet Jupiter's. The following night I switched it up, sitting beneath a dryer for hours, a dozen juice cans pinned atop my head. Each morning, I trotted off to 8 a.m. class, a picture perfect Ali MacGraw. Victory was short-lived; foiled by humidity and the invincibility of natural curl. By mid-afternoon, I trudged home, Roseanne Roseannadana's twin.

As college turned to career, I enlisted mercenaries, the professional hair stylists. My first recruit was Mario the Magnificent, hairdresser to the "stars". [In Hartford, this borders on hyperbole. Mario cut the hair of the local news anchor.] With flowing black hair, beard, and mustache, Mario [Lord forgive me, a really hot Jesus] was master of the silent snip. He never spoke, but every four weeks he accepted a week's worth of my pay to cut my hair to within two inches of my scalp. Apparently, Mario's battle plan was retreat. A long line of replacements followed: Mr. Paul, Mr. Joseph, Mr. Mister, and the ultimate turncoat, who shall remain nameless. Mr. No Name looked me right in my eye, "What do you care if your hair is too curly? Because, really, your face is nothing special."

Was Mr. No Name related to Paulie Poopalotti?

At the century's turn, my D-Day approached. Missy, a new aide-de-camp/hairstylist, led the final, triumphant charge against my life-long nemesis. Armed with industrial strength straightening gel and a sizzling, ionic titanium flat iron, she stamped out each wild curl, pressing the coiled tendrils into silken submission. My private war was over. Jubilant, I banished the relics of my six-decade struggle, oversized combs, brushes, and beautician egos. Yet, one memory lurked.

I spied him across the room at a class reunion. Wiry and skinny no more, Paulie Poopalotti barreled toward me, bellowing, "Is that Gina, the girl I tormented?" Paulie had enjoyed one plate of linguini or rotini too many. Removing the flabby arm that he had flung around my waist, I flicked a sleek tress out of my eyes. "Paul-ie, did you torment me? I don't remember that!" It may have cost me years of therapy and crates of Dippity-Do, but I finally saw the dawn's early light. With a name like Poopalotti, Paulie should have been more like Mario. He should have kept his mouth shut.

Phone Folly

A phone call in the middle of the night is *never* a good thing. On a mid-September night, I fall into an easy sleep, secure in the thought that my daughter Catherine is settling into college life. A rude ring rouses me. Mother's intuition, fueled by my overactive, overprotective gene, shoots into overdrive. I brace for bad news as my husband, Mr. Don't Worry Be Happy, picks up the phone.

"Hey, Catherine, how ya doing? Good. Yeah, Mom's right here."

It's midnight. Where did she think I'd be? At the mall? Out for cocktails?

"OK. I'll tell Mom. Have a good evening, now."

Have a good evening, now? Is he talking to his one and only baby daughter, away, alone, afraid...or the cashier at Stop & Shop?

"Catherine wants you to read your email."

"She called at midnight to tell me to read my email?"

Are you kidding me?

Fool that I am, I kick off the sheets, find my slippers, and shuffle off to my computer. Her message downloads.

Subject line: Question

Text: My stomach is a little upset and I was wondering what I should take for it. Some Pepto or Immodium or just ginger ale? Please call.

For a moment, I wonder if this is some kind of freshman hazing stunt; a dare to do something well, just stupid. What other reason would there be for her to call the land line to ask her father to tell her mother to read her email, an email in which she asks her mother to call her cell phone? Now is not the time to crack the DaVinci code, so I take the bait, place the call. My daughter is indeed experiencing mild stomach distress. Relieved that nothing is really wrong, I recommend a remedy and say goodnight. Sleep eludes me as I struggle to comprehend the cause for such convoluted communication. I toss and turn, remembering another late-night call.

I drop off Catherine at a sleepover involving twelve of her eight-year-old classmates. While I am sure this scenario has all the markings of imminent disaster, the perky mom-in-charge assures me that she "has it all under control." She will call if any problem arises. I spy the sheet pan of Rice Krispie treats, the table loaded with markers, glue, glitter, and sequins. In the family room, a gaggle of little girls stares at the TV, mesmerized by a Mary Kate and Ashley video. It will be alright. Triumphing over my overactive, overprotective gene, I head home, where the phone does not ring. Until three a.m. Caller ID flashes "Perky Mom."

"Get up Jeff, you'll have to go get Catherine. She must be sick, homesick, whatever...Come *on*, please get up and get going."

As I pick up the receiver, my husband reluctantly rises, throwing on a jacket, shoes, and the always necessary golf cap, ready to retrieve our daughter.

"Hi, Mom. It's me, Catherine."

I must tell her that "Hi, Mom" suffices. She is an only child. Who else would call me Mom?

"Catherine, honey, what's wrong?"

"Nothing, whatcha doing?"

"What am **I** doing? Well, I was sleeping, Catherine. What are **you** doing?" I hold up my index finger to Jeff, signaling him to stay put for the moment.

"Not too much. The girls thought we should call up one of our moms to say hi. I said 'Let's call my mom. She won't get mad!'"

Are you kidding me?

Not all alarming phone calls arrive in the wee hours of the morning. I am watching television on a mid-July evening when Catherine, interning in New York City, interrupts three times in short succession.

"Hi, Mom. It's me, Catherine." Mom, my friends and I are having a picnic at the outdoor movies at Bryant Park tomorrow night. I'm making tuna sandwiches. How much mayo should I put in?"

"Well, honey, it's a matter of taste. Depends how moist you like the tuna. Just be sure to keep them very cold. It's hot outside. They could spoil, you could get sick."

Overactive, overprotective gene at full throttle. I return to my show...for only a moment, until call #2.

"Mom, what should I put in the tuna salad?"

"Celery's good."

"I don't have any celery. How about a chopped up red pepper?"

I tell Catherine red pepper will replace celery nicely. I wish her a good night. Not quite yet. Last call.

"OK Mom, I opened the tuna fish can. One more thing. How do I cook it?"

Are you kidding me?

GINA T. BROADBENT

December's Forgotten Friend

Mid-December. I drive home from trip #126 to the mall, listening to the all-holiday-music, all-the-time radio station, tearing up as Sinatra croons "Faithful friends who are dear to us, gather near to us once more." Ah, I am a sentimental sap. Stopping at my mailbox to pick up the day's delivery of cards and bills [Yes, bills. It was trip #126 trip to the mall.], I am unfazed that the number of bills eclipses the number of cards. I keep that friends-and-family vibe going as I open cards only, calling out the names of each sender to my semi-interested husband. "Oh, isn't this nice! Joe, Joan, and Jenny sent us a card this year." Mere moments pass, and my husband actually responds, "Do we know Joe, Joan, and Jenny?" I ignore that Mr. Bah Humbug has failed to recognize Joe, the eldest of my nine cousins in Ohio, whom he met briefly at a funeral several years ago. I move quickly in and out of the playroom to stash away today's purchases, careful not to acknowledge the object of my most intense love-hate relationship, our bond cemented by 25 minutes of quality time together, several days a week. Yes, we are quite close; close in every month but December. Ah, I am a fickle friend. I will be sorry that, distracted by holiday frenzy, I have forgotten all about...my elliptical.

New Year's Day. I think about making amends. Just last night, I sang "Should auld acquaintance be forgot and never brought to mind." Although I find the meaning of these lyrics obscure, I assume that my resolution is to honor long-held friendships. But I am just too busy for my little "friend," covered with cobwebs and hidden away in the corner of the playroom like Rochester's mad wife in the attic. I am busy, un-decking the halls, making trip #145 back to the mall to exchange the gifts purchased on trip #132, and polishing off the last of the Christmas cookies. Reckoning is inevitable and, like a prodigal daughter, I cozy up to the elliptical, clearing away the rolls of wrapping paper and ribbon and empty boxes that keep it from my sight. We'll be back together, but first I will pay for my neglect.

Mid-January. Martin Luther King Day, and I too have a dream! A dream that I will be able to zip up my new size 6 wool skirt before April arrives. A dream that I will not, no questions asked, receive the senior citizen's discount at the movies. A dream that I will not have to wear Spanx under my golf skirt this summer. The rapprochement with my elliptical begins. As with so many reconciliations, it is tentative, cautious at first. I stroke away the dust from its front panel and gaze at its gages; from speedometer to pedometer to caloric register. I inch in closer, positioning my feet and pressing my full (and since our last rendezvous, increased) weight on the pedals. At first, the elliptical is unforgiving. It resists my efforts, paying me back with pain in my every step. Attempting to mask the awkwardness of my prolonged absence, I plug in my headphones and try to lose myself in the music. I forge on, knowing that this relationship is worth it. I catch my breath, wipe my brow, and begin to hit full stride. If I could sing, I would sing; just like Peaches and Herb, "Reunited and it feels so good."

Past My Bedtime

Sleeping is one of my favorite activities. Yes, sleeping is an activity. Before sweeping this assertion under the mattress with other overused, tired oxymorons like jumbo shrimp, consider the following: A person, contingent upon weight, metabolism, the temperature of the room, and the alignment of the stars, can burn 500 calories during eight blissful hours of sleep. This same person, again subject to an array of variables, can burn 500 calories during a single, strenuous and sweaty hour of jogging, stair-stepping, or cycling. Hamlet may have wrung his hands, mumbling "to sleep, perchance to dream." I clap my hands, shouting "Now I lay me down to sleep, bag of Doritos at my feet."

The ability to lose while I snooze makes me want to sleep even more. But shuteye and I have not always been in love. George Bernard Shaw lamented "Youth is wasted on the young." I counter that the gift of forty winks is frittered away on four-year-olds. Like most children, I fussed at naps and rebelled at enforced, early bedtimes. Showing signs of what would be a life-long affliction of naïveté, I believed my fourth-grade classmates, who, crossing their hearts and hoping to die, told me that they stayed up for Johnny Carson every night. These were the same classmates who watched in delight as my head bent backwards at a ninety-degree angle when they told me the word "gullible" was written on the ceiling. I lobbied my mother, to no avail, for a later bedtime. She mortified me by telling my friends who telephoned after 9 p.m. that I was in bed. I begged her to say simply that I, like any normal ten-year-old, "had stepped out for the evening." She refused to budge an inch, condemning me to everlasting babyhood. Powerless to prevail for a commutation of my early-bedtime sentence, I chose to control the terms of my imprisonment.

Showing signs of what would become a life-long affliction of "just a little bit neurotic," I followed ten easy steps to a happy bedtime. Step one: Shut, or preferably slam, my bedroom door at 9 p.m. Step two: Firmly close my closet door against the errant monsters, uninvited aliens, and spooks in the night that lurked behind it. Step three: Check under the bed for additional monsters, aliens, and spooks. Step four: Refuse the offer of the wardens, more commonly called Mom and Dad, who knocked on the door offering to tuck me in. No, thank you. I would handle my own turn-down service. Anyway, why did my mother even bother? Didn't she need to be free to work the phones and ensure my humiliation by announcing to the fourth grade that I was already under the covers? Step five: Pull back the bedspread and carefully fold several inches of top sheet over the blanket. Step six: Tightly insert the top sheet and blanket in between mattress and box spring. Step seven: Crouch against the headboard and slide feet first between top and bottom sheet, savoring their soft, cool touch. Step eight. Switch off bedside lamp. Step nine: Call out "Mom, Dad, can you turn on my night light?" "Can I have a kiss goodnight?" Step ten: Pray the phone does not ring.

Fast forward seven years. There was no bedtime or box spring. There were seldom clean sheets and rarely a good night's sleep. I had entered the twilight zone where day turned into night without a perceptible change in the activity of the zone's inhabitants, who roamed with the hollow, glassy-eyed look that came of one too many "all-nighters" spent studying or partying. I lived in the land of sleep deprivation. I lived in a college dorm. How could I just be going to bed when the birds were already singing? My dear mother, the poster child for the importance of sleep, had little sympathy, but rather an uncanny affinity for phone calls at the nine o'clock hour. She phoned me at 9 a.m. on a spring morning at the end of my senior year. "My god, Mother, I was sleeping! You woke me up." I was reluctant to reveal that I had returned from "stepping out for the evening" only a few hours earlier. "All right dear; go back to sleep. Enjoy sleeping the day away while you can. It will change."

Change it did. Fast forward fifteen years. There was no bedtime because there was no time for bed. I had traveled far beyond the twilight zone into the outer limits where night and day existed, but I could not tell the difference. I was ruled by the conflicting demands of a wailing, seven-pound blob of precious flesh and my primal, unattainable desire for two hours of uninterrupted sleep. I was the mother of a newborn. One dimly lit, bird-chirping dawn, my husband and I bumped into each other on the staircase, each drunk from too little sleep. As he descended to go to work, I ascended to flop into bed after an "all-nighter" of nursing and nodding off at David Letterman and his late night and late-late night pals. I excused my husband's keen insight into the obvious, "My god, I never knew sleep meant so much to me!" Good ole' mom, captain of the sleep police, had been right all along. Enjoy it while you can. As I finally tucked in my baby girl, switched on the night light, and kissed her good night, I prayed the phone would not ring.

My One True Love

I've never met a carb I didn't like. While I recognize a certain elitist élan surrounding the rail-thin, radiant women who, nose in air, proclaim "I do not eat carbs," I revel in my love affair with the carbohydrate. Simple or complex, starchy or fibrous, good or bad; I love them all! The carb has never let me down, bringing me indescribable moments of ecstasy with a single bite of a red velvet cupcake. Oh, but I have been fickle. Even when the carbohydrate has shed its low-life sugary companions to hang out with the virtuous vitamins in an organic apple, I have turned away. Why, not once, not twice, but, lo, three times, did I break up with my one true love, "my Carb"?

Carb and I first parted company when I was desperate; desperate to fit into my skinny jeans by the end of the week. My hairdresser, always a sound source for nutritional advice, told me about a then-new diet trend in which the pounds just "fell off." I needed my jeans to all but fall off, so I asked for details.

"It's a great diet, some doctor made it up. His name is Adams, Atwood...Atkins, that's it! Well, anyway, the thing is you can eat all the meat, all the fat, you want. Just no carbs. No bread, not even fruit. It's great. Like, I mean, you can eat a whole roast chicken, skin and all, for dinner!"

That should have stopped me. When had I ever wanted to eat a whole roast chicken, skin and all? Somehow, the thought of devouring a whole roast anything brought Henry VIII to mind. I had an inkling of what happened to the women who ate dinner with him. But there I was, losing my head over a weight loss scheme. I stocked up on hamburger, steak, blue cheese dressing, and, yes, even pork rinds and beef jerky. Yum! It was fun at first. I hadn't had blue cheese dressing in years. Sure enough, come Saturday, after I sucked in my stomach and lay flat on my bed, I was able to zip up my jeans. Within three weeks, I could put on those same jeans like a normal person before heading out for dinner. Sad to say, I didn't want dinner. If I ate one more burger (no bun) and iceberg with blue cheese, I would scream. I had a little taste of a chocolate chip cookie. I nibbled on a few grapes. I ate a sandwich! Reconciling with Carb, I confessed, "It was all wrong. Wrong from the start. I couldn't go on any longer with Dr. Atkins. I can't give you up!" Carb came back, and so did the pounds.

Year after year, I found fulfillment with my Carb. Was it midlife crisis? Was it insanity? Or was it that ever present Catholic guilt that drove me to a second separation, a long forty-day and forty-night separation, from Carb? I gave up "sweets" for Lent. Carb would stay in my life, in pasta, in pears, in pizza. I denied myself the parts of Carb I loved best, the cakes, the cookies, the candy. I was distancing myself for a righteous reason; not for the vanity of too tight jeans, but for a passport to Paradise. I persevered through the first weeks, shutting off the television when a Chips Ahoy commercial appeared. An Italian girl, I welcomed St. Patrick's Day like never before. On March 17, smack in the middle of Lent, the Church decreed a one-day hiatus to all sacrifice and denial. If you had given up alcohol, have a drink. If you had given up cigarettes, have a smoke. If March 17 falls on a Friday, have a steak! Or, better yet, have a little corned beef. Gobbling up all sweets in sight, I took full advantage of this day of dispensation. As Lent's forty days faded, along with my fortitude, I learned another nugget of Catholic dogma. My dry cleaner, a highly reliable source of theological information, advised that fasting ended not on Easter morning, but blessedly at noon on Holy Saturday. Hallelujah! As if I had heard it from the Pope himself, at precisely noon on the Saturday before Easter I was on the doorstep of my favorite bakery. Cramming down a cannoli, my separation with Carb was over.

My devotion continued even as a barrage of accusations and innuendos swirled about Carb. So-called "experts" [most likely the brainless fools who advocated consuming large quantities of pork rinds and beef jerky to lose weight] labeled Carb as empty, especially when Carb got together with wine. This was hitting below the belt, [assuming that I complemented my elastic-waist slacks with a belt]. Wine was second only to Carb in my affection. How blasphemous to describe wine, Carb, or, worse, a wine glass as empty! I vowed undying loyalty to Carb. A new Lenten season approached, and with it, a nagging need to sacrifice. Surely, I could forgo pleasure for a couple of weeks [actually 5.7 weeks, but who's counting?]. I would do it. I would give it up.

My husband had no intention of suffering himself during Lent. "Don't, don't do it! No way. Please don't do it. I swear to God, I can't live in this house if you do!"

I gave up wine for Lent. To those at whom I may have glared or grunted during this forty-day period, I apologize. I missed empty Carb even more than sweet Carb. At precisely noon on the Saturday before Easter, I was popping that cork and filling that empty wine glass.

Another Four-Letter Word

I recently added a new four-letter word to my repertoire. Although this word can be fraught with as much anger and angst as the garden-variety expletive deleted, it is generally accepted for use in polite conversation.

The word? Golf.

Never a gifted athlete, I took up the sport ten or maybe fifteen years ago. My husband spent the greater part of each weekend attempting to loft a little white ball into the air and land it as close as possible, if in fact not directly into, an almost-as-little tin cup. Humans indeed pursue strange activities, but if you can't beat 'em, join 'em. Ever the optimist, I was sure that accompanying my husband on the fairway could only strengthen our marriage, even bring us closer. [More on that little pipedream later.] Ever the material girl, I was excited to expand my wardrobe with cute shorts, skorts, and assorted accessories straight out of a Garanimals catalog. Better yet, my golfing friends assured me that at the end of nine holes, at least one fine glass of wine awaited. Fore!

A few lessons under my belt and I was ready to go. Bedecked in a chartreuse and pink checked skirt, white polo shirt with coordinating chartreuse and pink checked collar, and white ankle socks trimmed in, you guessed it, chartreuse and pink checks, I climbed into the golf cart. Jeff and I were off on our first official round of golf together! First hole. I turned out a decent drive, fair fairway shots, weak chipping, and a putrid putt. Jeff gushed with praise for my less-than-remarkable game. I cast him a sideways glance, fully expecting to see him waving pom poms in the air and executing a perfect backflip. "Good shot, hon!" "Nice try!" "Oops, that's too bad." His rendition of the Hallelujah Chorus continued for the next few holes. Hey, maybe I am good at this, after all! By the fifth hole, there is change in the air, the slightest of shifts in the earth's epicenter as the perky cheerleader morphs into stern schoolmaster. "Keep your head down." "Bring your club back farther." "Follow through." I made these corrections as my balls veered into the woods, landed in the sand, plopped into the pond. Oh, the unspoken thoughts as the teacher droned on. "Choke up on the club." "I may choke you." "Watch your ball." "Watch yours." "Move your legs wider apart." "Excuse me?" At last, the final hole. I channeled the sincerity of Jeff's early flattery by exclaiming, "Honey, that was so much fun! Where's the wine?"

It was one long hot summer. Weekend after weekend, we hit the links. I was no longer Jeff's silent student. The quiet words that echoed in my head now exploded from my mouth. "You know this is par if you make the putt." *"Great, jinx me so I'll miss it."* I miss it. "Play the break." "Too much club." "You are lined up all wrong." *"Will you please shut the [another four- letter word] up?"* At least I said please. Jeff no longer called me "hon" or "sweetie" on the golf course. He opted for a new term of endearment, Godzilla, symbolic of the vigor with which I chipped and putt. I tended to overshoot the green and land on the next tee box. While his pet name drew laughs from fellow golfers, I was not amused. I became amused, though, when I summoned that same Godzilla-like subtlety to outdrive my husband. Ever the lady, I refrained from gloating. "Can you believe my ball went farther than yours? Maybe you didn't follow through."

Summer ended. Our marriage did not. The loving rivalry continued golf season after golf season. Suddenly, there was yet another slight shift in the earth's epicenter. For one very brief, very shining moment, Godzilla Gina became Birdie Broadbent. We approached a par three hole on a perfect mid-August Friday evening. My drive landed on the green, two feet from the cup. Having learned many summers ago not to point out the obvious chance for a birdie, Jeff stood quietly back. My Godzilla gene in check, I gently made the putt. I was rewarded by the sound of the ball draining into the hole. "Great putt. Congratulations, hon." Next Friday evening, same hole. I swept away all thoughts of a repeat performance. When my ball landed in the rough, 30 feet off the green, I was certain that lightning would not strike twice in the same place. I mouthed one of those four-letter words. Jeff decided that it was a good time to move the cart. Unobserved, I banished the king of the monsters to chip the ball right into the hole. Bring it on!

Summer follows summer. Good shots follow bad shots, bringing forth so many of those unacceptable four-letter words to the tips of so many tongues. Ever the optimist, I like to dream about the elusive hole in one. And I like to think about my favorite four-letter words: golf, wine, and, oh yes, Jeff.

Fan-tastic Fears!

I am not a fan of elevators. Conventional wisdom contends that moving up in life is a good thing. I disagree, at least when it comes to elevators. Moving up is not good, moving down is not much better, and moving out, right out the elevator door, is best of all. I avoid the elevator at all costs, opting to scale flight after flight of stairs rather than cross into that cramped cage. Really, what's the difference? Either way, I arrive at my destination, gasping for breath, gagging from nausea, and gleaming with sweat. Call me claustrophobic, control freak, or just freaking crazy, just don't call me into an elevator. Despite my best efforts to run, not walk, to any staircase in sight, inevitably a god-forsaken moment arises when I have no choice but to hop onboard. Why is it, at this very moment, that 39 other people decide to file into the same elevator with a posted capacity of 40? Why is it, at this very moment, that countless 21st century Sir Galahads crawl out of the woodwork, insisting "ladies first" as they push me to the rear of the torture chamber? No! No! No! I must enter last. I must stand as close as possible to the front, even if my nose touches the elevator door. While there is still time to escape, I run down my list of safety checks. Emergency phone? Alarm button? Certificate of inspection, preferably time stamped within the previous three hours? As the two slabs of steel shut tight, I draw in all of my breath, letting it out bit by bit as the red lights signal that we've landed on the second floor, the third floor, the fourth floor, and finally, mercifully, the desired floor. I distract myself from the endless seconds that pass until the doors part, praying, "Jesus, have pity on me, a poor sinner." My hand moves in a frantic circular motion, like a police officer directing cars through a construction site, as I will the doors to open. Open they do. I am relieved, but only temporarily, for what goes up, must go down. I am not a fan of repeat performances.

I am a fan of the aisle seat, claiming it as my own whenever TicketMaster and the good Lord permit. TicketMaster obliges. Might there be an asterisk after my name in its database: "Do Not Assign Middle Seat"? After all, TicketMaster might or might not have fielded some complaints when I was forced to sit in the dead center of the row. Was it wrong that I squirmed throughout the entire two hours and fifty minutes of *Les Mis*? Was it wrong that I urged my seatmates to forget about that cry-baby Jean Valjean and his lousy loaf of bread and to focus instead on my misery? Was it wrong that I nudged, ever so slightly, the white-haired woman with the walker as I dashed to the door before any of that "Bravo" or, worse yet, "Encore" stuff began? TicketMaster and I have an understanding. No aisle seat, no tickie.

The good Lord apparently really meant, "The first shall be last." Sure enough, every Sunday, I arrive early at church to snag a seat snug against the end of the pew. Sure enough, every Sunday a good Catholic family of six arrives well after Mass has started.

The usher approaches me. "Move in, please." I try to step out into the aisle, allowing the two parents and four sniffling kids to climb over me into the center of the pew.

The usher is adamant. "Come on, Ma'am, move in."

The choir launches into "Let There Be Peace on Earth." It is the wrong time for a scene. I scoot in, finding myself wedged between an elderly gentleman who has ingested significant amounts of garlic, and one of the sniffling kids, who has wiped all manner of flu, Covid, and possibly bubonic plague germs onto his clammy palm. Why doesn't hand sanitizer flow from the baptismal font? I am a fan of Purell.

I am not a fan of boxes, especially when box is merely a euphemism for eternal resting place. Given my aversion to enclosed elevator spaces and my preference for easy-exit aisle seats, it should come as no surprise that I am deathly [well, yeah!] afraid of being laid to rest. My husband appeals to decades of ingrained catechism and rationality [ha!]. "But, Gina, you're a good religious girl. It's just your soul that lives on. You won't feel 'boxed' in."

I have pledged to haunt him if he tries to bury me. I will not torment him with namby-pamby, garden variety spooky stuff like creaking doors, flickering lights, or howling winds. I want to hit him where it hurts. I'll make the chocolate chip cookies disappear to a place he fears, the nether land near the vacuum cleaner. I'll interrupt the internet connection in the last three seconds of the NCAA championship. He'll see the error of his ways. In a heartbeat, he'll be spreading my ashes over my happy place, the parking lot at Talbot's.

I am a fan of Talbot's.

Milton Keynes UK
Ingram Content Group UK Ltd.
UKHW052233051224
452053UK00008B/104

* 9 7 9 8 9 9 1 8 2 8 1 1 6 *